SAFe® PI Planning

A Step-By-Step Guide

A Step-By-Step Guide To PI Planning using the Scaled Agile Framework

By Liam Kane

Fourth Edition

Published by Agile One Media, LLC

Additional help and resources related to this book can be found at
http://www.agileonemedia.com.

ISBN: 9781717711809

Printed in the United States of America

Contents

Foreword 7

1.   Introduction to SAFe 15

     The SAFe Big Picture - Simplified...................19

     3-Level SAFe Summary 20

     Summary of SAFe Operating Levels: 24

     SAFe Process Flow Summary 24

     Prerequisites for Adopting SAFe......................30

2.   SAFe Portfolio Management 33

     Definitions 33

     Portfolio Management Inputs & Outputs 39

     Creating a Portfolio Backlog 40

     The Portfolio Kanban 43

     Managing Portfolio Delivery.............................48

     Portfolio Review..49

Portfolio Management Team Roles 51

Key Portfolio Management Ceremonies 53

Portfolio Management Checklist 54

3.   Constructing A Program Backlog 55

Feature Intake Kanban 57

Feature Intake Kanban Operation 61

Feature Intake Roles and Responsibilities 62

Ranking Features With WSJF 63

Feature Definition Template 64

Feature Intake Process Checklist 66

4.   The PI Planning Event 67

Introduction 67

PI Planning Goals 67

Day 1 - Draft Plans 71

Creating User Stories from Features 71

Story And Feature Size Estimates 76

Story & Feature Scheduling..............................80

Setting Team PI Objectives...............................85

Team Risk Assessments....................................86

The End of the Iron Triangle.............................87

Draft Plan Presentations.................................88

Leadership Review And Problem Solving 88

Day 2 - Finalizing Plans 89

Planning Updates 89

Consolidated Program Wall Board 90

Scoring PI Objectives 93

Final Plan Reviews 94

Team Risk Review...95

Team Confidence Vote....................................96

Program Risk Review......................................97

Program Confidence Vote 97

Event Retrospective......................................98

PI Objectives Rollup and Event Close 99

PI Planning Process Summary..99

5.   PI Execution Practices 103

Program Synchronization 105

Scrum of Scrums (ART Sync)..107

Measuring Program Progress..111

Program-Level Inspect and Adapt...................................115

Integrating Scrum into SAFe..116

PI Execution Checklist 121

Final Thoughts...123

About The Author 125

Recommended Reading..127

Index..129

Foreword

To hear it told is not the same as experience.

- Chinese Proverb

Scrum is one of the most successful frameworks for agile software development by teams of 5-9 people. Scrum's empirical approach mitigates against many of the problems encountered with traditional software development methods. It's short inspect and adapt cycles support incremental and iterative development. Scrum provides a structure that includes roles, practices and artifacts whereby teams can build shippable product increments in short iterations called sprints. Many enterprises however frequently struggle to scale scrum beyond the individual team level, and quickly discover that additional operating practices are needed to plan and coordinate the work for large, multi-team projects. Since the construction of much real-world, commercial-scale software requires development capacities well in excess of a single scrum team, the scaling challenge is both very real and pervasive. Furthermore, even in cases where small numbers of teams are engaged in constructing product solutions, there is still a necessity for a set of interconnected practices that transform business strategy into working products in a continuous flow with minimum delays

7

and waste between the operating levels within an enterprise. Several frameworks have emerged over recent years to tackle the scaling challenge, and Dean Leffingwell's *Scaled Agile Framework (SAFe)* has established itself as one of the most popular and widely adopted. SAFe is not only about doing scrum on a large scale, but defines additional practices for each of the generic operating levels within an enterprise: Business Strategy and Portfolio Management, Program Management, and Delivery Team practices. Hence SAFe is concerned with the scaling both horizontally (multiple collaborating delivery teams) and vertically (continuous flow of work from business strategy to working software). The goal is full end-to-end business agility with practices aimed at ensuring solid alignment between business and delivery teams.

SAFe is not without its criticisms, not least of which are its large-scale up-front planning process, its top-down, highly structured approach and its perceived emphasis on process over people. SAFe however provides a comprehensive solution to the scaling challenge. Hence its appeal to large organizations and the risk-averse executives who run them. There is no doubt that in the hands of an unenlightened leadership team it has the potential to be mis-used in the service of command-and-control. Nonetheless, most leaders do 'get it', embrace the lean principles behind it, and are happy to get out of the way and focus on their real roles – painting a compelling vision, and supporting their teams through training, productive workspaces, promoting a positive work environment, and providing opportunities for individual growth.

SAFe is a large, complex and evolving framework, and although it is well-defined in terms of practices, roles and artifacts, there is no prescribed implementation strategy, and organizations are instead encouraged to engage the services of SAFe Program Consultants (SPCs – trained and certified by Scaled Agile Inc.) to provide implementation guidance and coaching. SAFe comes with a large and expensive learning curve. Many SAFe supporters will argue that SAFe is so simple it can be described by a single chart – the SAFe Big Picture chart! I don't find this very convincing, and do not know anyone who can look at this chart and walk away claiming they understand SAFe. SAFe comes with its own unique and arcane lexicon of Agile Release Trains, Program Increments and Architectural Runways. It takes time to understand these concepts, decide which ones you need, and leverage them in an effective way to support the needs of your organization.

Keep in mind that SAFe, like scrum, is a *framework*, not a prescription, and must be tailored to meet the unique needs of every organization. Thus, organizations should not attempt a wholesale adoption of the entire framework – this is unnecessary, and a recipe for becoming overwhelmed in complexity, risk and inevitable failure. The key question is – what are the core practices needed to get started - what is the simplest thing that could possibly work? Is there a simple baseline pattern, or template, that can be used as a starting point, but still solves many of the practical challenges of scaling?

Bottom line: If I were selecting a vendor from whom to purchase a major software application or solution, I'd be inclined to go with one who had adopted a recognizable framework over one with a set of ad hoc practices. At least then I could communicate using an established vocabulary, and should have the confidence that a measurable set of objectives were being met on a frequent cadence.

This book is the result of my own firsthand experiences in helping organizations to scale. My aim is to save you time, effort and expense by providing a clear and easy guide to the SAFe framework, to arm you with the knowledge to engage productively with SAFe consultants, and to equip you to better articulate your scaling needs and the scope of a solution. For those who want to jump right in and begin building or experimenting with their own implementation, this book is a hands-on, step-by-step guide to get you started.

SAFe® and Scaled Agile Framework are registered trademarks of Scaled Agile Inc.

How This Book Is Organized

Chapter 1. Introduction to the Scaled Agile Framework, provides an overview of the SAFe framework and the lean principles behind it.

Chapter 2. SAFe Portfolio Management, describes the operation of the highest level of SAFe and shows how business strategy can be translated into a set of realizable program deliverables.

Chapter 3. Constructing A Program Backlog. The Program Backlog is the starting point for PI Planning, and it is crucial to get this step right. This chapter describes how to create a ranked list of features, sufficiently well-defined to support PI Planning.

Chapter 4. PI Planning Step-By-Step, takes you through each of the basic steps of planning a Program Increment.

Chapter 5. PI Execution Practices, explains the essential roles, practices and artifacts necessary for successful execution of a Program Increment by multiple synchronized teams.

Frequent use of sidebars is made throughout the book where a deeper dive into selected topics is warranted.

1. Introduction to SAFe

In any enterprise that produces software for sale to external customers, or for internal consumption in support of business operations, the transformation of business needs to working software flows through three basic processing levels: Portfolio-Program-Delivery. The work to be undertaken at each level is captured in a backlog (portfolio backlog, program backlog, team backlog), from where it is pulled for processing. Completed work is subjected to an *Inspect and Adapt* (or, *Check and Adjust*) process, which acts as part of a feedback loop that serves to enable course corrections within any of the three levels. End-to-end agility is achieved by maintaining a continuous flow of work from strategy formulation all the way to product deployment, with minimal delays between each of the processing levels, and feedback loops designed to enable rapid course corrections and adjustments.

Business Strategy And Portfolio Management: Each business unit within an enterprise will have a *portfolio* of revenue-generating (or revenue-supporting) products and/or services. A *portfolio* is a collection of programs or products managed as a group to achieve strategic objectives, and *Portfolio Management* is the centralized management of one or more portfolios to achieve those objectives. Portfolio management is basically about deciding which initiatives to implement and in what order or priority. In SAFe, the initiatives selected to implement strategy are packaged as *epics*. Epics typically require multiple releases (or *program increments*) to bring to full realization. Epics are basically containers for everything needed to provide a solution. Each epic should have a vision, roadmap and MVP (minimum viable product) definition. Once epics are fully defined and approved at the portfolio level, they are added to the *portfolio backlog*, from where they are pulled by programs and delivered incrementally via a series of Program Increments (PI's), each typically spanning a 10-12-week time-box. Epics in the business portfolio are refined via an intake workflow using a *kanban* which is used to steer individual epics through a series of workflow states, each representing increasing stages of refinement. (More about this in Chapter 3). Each of the levels in the SAFe framework, including portfolio management, is intended to operate as a feedback loop. This is the heart of empirical method: Plan-Do-Check-Adjust (or, Build-Measure-Learn). If business agility is about going from idea to delivered value as quickly as possible, then a fast feedback loop at the portfolio level is essential for ensuring rapid adjustment of strategy in response to the changing demands of customers and the market environment.

Program Management: At this level we are working to translate individual business initiatives (epics) into tangible product features that can be built by development teams. Our planning granularity is at the level of features, and our estimates are based on team velocities (team production capacities). We employ mechanisms to ensure that business stakeholders and delivery teams are fully aligned on business outcomes and value. Our tracking granularity is at the feature level and we use a program-level PDCA cycle to respond to emerging program risks ensuring that maximum business value is preserved. The primary goal of the program level is to maximize the delivery of value. To do this, epics are elaborated into product features that are refined using a feature intake Kanban until they are deemed *ready* for consumption by delivery teams. Features that have been refined to this state of readiness are considered part of the *program backlog*. To derive a viable PI Plan, program backlog items are broken down into iteration-sized pieces called *user stories* and estimated. Knowledge of team velocities is then used to estimate the scope of what can be delivered in a PI.

Delivery Team Operations: Teams produce features incrementally via short iterations that deliver production-quality code. Most teams use the *scrum framework* to accomplish this: sprint planning, daily stand-ups, sprint reviews and sprint retrospectives to deliver working subsets of their PI objectives every two weeks. Additional practices like TDD, test automation are used to ensure that quality is built into every iteration.

When people ask, 'why do we need a scaling framework', they are usually looking for a solution to the above set of needs, none of which are addressed directly by Scrum, or XP, or Kanban.

There are several scaling frameworks available to help with these challenges: Large-Scale Scrum (LeSS), Disciplined Agile Delivery (DAD), Agile@Scale, and the Scaled Agile Framework (SAFe), each with its own practices, roles, artifacts and associated jargon. Either one of these frameworks can be adopted to help organizations scale their team-level agile practices. So why pick SAFe? SAFe has established itself as the most widely adopted of the scaling frameworks and, according to their website, over 70 percent of US Fortune 100 companies have trained practitioners and consultants. Access to certified training and support resources is widely available, and this factor can substantially improve the likelihood of successful adoption.

SAFe is a framework for developing software at scale using agile and lean principles. The framework defines a set of practices, roles and artifacts for each of the generic operating levels within an enterprise. Work flows from one level to the next with increasing levels of refinement. One level of the framework is connected to the next via a backlog from which ready work is pulled for processing. The overall goal is that work flows without interruption or delay between levels. This is accomplished by balancing the load represented by each backlog with the available capacity of the consuming operating level. One of the pillars of the 'SAFe House of Lean' is the principle of *flow*, which is defined as '*Optimize continuous and sustainable throughput of value* '. Continuous flow is a fundamental part of the SAFe model. This is accomplished via a sequence of interconnected kanbans that operate continuously, and ultimately feed delivery teams with a steady flow of ready work.

The SAFe Big Picture - Simplified

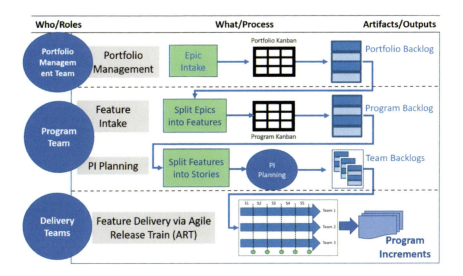

The SAFe Big Picture, Simplified

For most organizations, that is, those with individual programs that can be delivered by 5-12 teams (< 125 people per program), 3-level SAFe suffices to cover their needs. For organizations with very large programs requiring multiple release trains per program, the SAFe Large Solution configuration is required. This configuration has additional roles, artifacts and events, focused on managing and coordinating the work of multiple Agile Release Trains.

The majority of organizations should be able to operate with 3-level SAFe (Portfolio, Program, and Team levels). Within the 3-

level operating model, each level has its own set of practices, roles and artifacts.

3-Level SAFe Summary

We can distill the SAFe Big Picture Diagram into a simpler version to show the basic flow of primary artifacts through the overall framework. This diagram, shown above, intentionally leaves out quite a bit of detail, so we can get a good grasp on how the overall process is intended to work from business strategy to working software.

3-level SAFe can be summarized as follows:

1. Portfolio Level:
   - Translate strategy into initiatives (Epics)
   - Epic Definition, Refinement, Prioritization
   - Approved epics in a Portfolio Backlog
2. Program Level
   - Elaboration of epics into features
   - Feature Definition & Refinement
   - A Program Backlog containing features deemed ready for consumption by delivery teams
   - PI Planning: A process to agree business objectives and scope for the next Program Increment
3. Team Level: PI Execution via Release Trains
   - Team agile practices (Scrum, XP, Kanban)

The SAFe Requirements Hierarchy

It can be useful to think of this framework flow as a cascading sequence of transformation patterns that runs continuously to convert business initiatives into working software. For this process to run smoothly, we need solid alignment between an organization's business leadership and its delivery teams. Here are additional views that may help visualize the relationship between Epics, Features and Stories:

SAFe Requirements Refinement

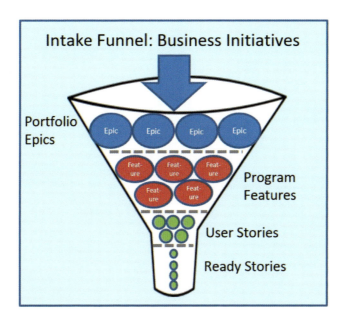

Epics are defined by business stakeholders and represent individual initiatives needed to implement strategy. Epics identify specific problems to be solved and provide a high level scope of the solution. Features represent solutions to the problems defined in the epics. Features provide capabilities or services to actual users. Delivery teams break features into iteration-sized pieces called user stories, and use them to build out features incrementally. Epics, Features and User Stories are stored in separate backlogs in each level of the SAFe hierarchy.

To put this in the context of SAFe levels and practices, the following diagram illustrates how a single epic might be delivered over 4 Program Increments:

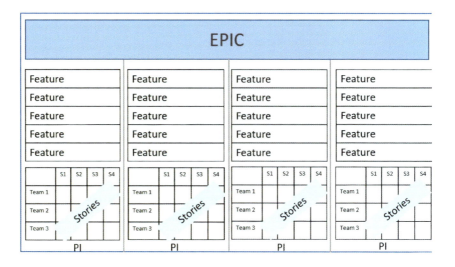

The SAFe Requirements Hierarchy

The business portfolio is represented as a backlog of *epics*. Epics typically take multiple PI's to fully realize. At the program level, epics are broken down into PI-sized pieces called *features*. Features are scoped and sized so they can be delivered in a single PI. Delivery

22

teams take features and break then into iteration-sized fragments called *user stories*. User Stories mare small slices of user functionality that can be delivered in single iterations.

Summary of SAFe Operating Levels:

- At the ***portfolio level***, business strategy is translated into initiatives represented by *epics*, that are then refined into sufficient detail that they can be consumed by program teams for elaboration into *features* that can be built and tested.
- At the ***program level***, features are fully defined in terms of benefits and acceptance criteria, and initial user stories are proposed (headline-level detail only).
- At the ***team level***, user stories are refined further (via backlog grooming/refinement) until they are sufficiently well-defined to be ready for implementation via sprints.

SAFe Process Flow Summary

Each stage of refinement delivers its output onto a backlog of items sufficiently refined to meet a definition of *ready* for consumption by the next level of the framework. Definitions of *Ready*, both at the epic and feature levels, have been proposed by the SAFe framework, in terms of templates. Epics require a vision (in elevator pitch format) and a list of required features/capabilities. For features, it is recommended that a list of benefits (why do we need this feature) and acceptance criteria are required for each one. The output of one set of practices feeds another via backlogs of ready work, realized as a series of interconnected *kanbans*.

All levels of the framework are intended to run concurrently, and largely independently. The flow between each level is managed by having backlogs appropriately sized for the capacity of the consuming level.

- SAFe uses 3 sets of interconnected backlogs:
  - Portfolio (Business Epics)
  - Program (Features)
  - Team (User Stories)
- Each represents increasing levels of detail – sufficient for consumption by next layer of the framework. (Templates exist for Epics, Features and User Stories).
- Each 'owned' and managed by a Product Owner:
  - Portfolio (Epic Owner(s))
  - Program (Product Manager)
  - Team (Team Product Owner)

The preceding has been a high-level summary of the steps required to get work defined, planned and delivered from business portfolio to working software. The question now is – what mechanics or governance mechanisms do we need to support these processes in a simple but consistent fashion. Each of the 3 major operational areas comprises a set of practices, artifacts, and roles. In what follows we will elaborate on each of these 3 parts of the framework.

A Word About Lean and Kanban

The concept of *lean* features prominently in the SAFe framework. Lean has its roots in the Toyota Production System (TPS), and it is ultimately about creating a culture of continuous improvement where all members of an organization are actively working to improve the performance of the business over time, the ultimate goal being the delivery of maximum value at minimum cost. Much has been written about lean and the literature frequently talks about the *House of Lean*, with its two, three, four, or more *pillars*. The SAFe version of the House of Lean has four pillars: respect for people and culture, flow, innovation and relentless improvement. Fundamentally, lean is really about two pillars:

- The practice of continuous improvement
- The power of respect for people

At Toyota, the meaning of the phrase "respect for people" encompasses building a culture where people want to improve, teaching them the tools for improvement, and motivating them to apply those tools every day. At Toyota they say: "We build people before we build cars."

Another common way to describe lean is the practice and process of identifying and removing waste. This is how we deliver maximum value at minimum cost, and a number of lean principles have been defined in support of this:

- Value – define value from the perspective of the customer
- Value Stream – define the sequence of process steps required to deliver value
- Flow – make the value stream *flow* – eliminate queues, bottlenecks, delays. Strive for the maximum sustainable throughput.
- Pull – pull only a quantity of work that the next downstream process can consume. (Managed by applying WIP constraints). If you overload the capacity of a workflow state, you slow things down.
- Perfection – continuously and relentlessly eliminate waste and strive to optimize the flow of value.

Kanban is a tool for managing *flow*. Kanban is a *pull-system* based on lean principles. At its core is the process of pulling individual work requests through a sequence of value-adding activities, smoothly and without interruption. The purpose of a Kanban is to:

- Bring visibility to both work and workflow (value and value stream. Note, many teams mistakenly believe that if they put cards on a board with columns they are doing Kanban. This is only the first step.
- Make process policies explicit. This means having definitions of *done* for every workflow state.
- Limit *work in progress*. Pull value through the value stream based on the capacity of each workflow step

27

(WIP). Do not overload workflow steps beyond their available capacity – this slows down the entire process.

- Manage flow. The goal is continuous and sustainable throughput of value.
- Measure and improve relentlessly: identify bottlenecks, waste, variability and remove them.

In scrum, pull means take the next set of items from the product backlog into a sprint where the amount of work selected matches the team's capacity. For Kanban, pull is applied at the level of each individual workflow state, and is controlled by WIP limits. In scrum, WIP is the quantity of work pulled for the whole sprint, and is equivalent to the team's *velocity*.

Teams will have a variety of maturity levels for their Kanban implementation. However, starting with an existing progress, teams can improve their depth of implementation. Both Kanban and scrum frameworks have built-in mechanisms (Plan-Do-Check-Adjust) for identifying and addressing issues that impact performance or impediments to the steady flow of value. Because they are both *pull systems*, they cannot be overloaded if their capacity is set appropriately, that is, they both support the maintenance of a sustainable pace.

The House of Lean:

Ultimate Goal-Value Delivery: Products and services that provide real value, have the highest quality, lowest cost and shortest lead times. Achieved via:

- **Respect for People**: Give teams autonomy on how their work gets done. Give people the tools, training, support, and work environment to succeed.
- **Continuous Improvement**. Relentlessly strive to identify and eliminate all sources of waste from the value stream. Tools such as PDCA – Plan, Do, Check and Adjust – are used.

Leadership: The foundation - responsible for the overall vision and for building and supporting the Respect for People and Continuous Improvement pillars.

The House of Lean

Prerequisites for Adopting SAFe

Here are some basic prerequisites that organizations should have in place before beginning a SAFe adoption. If these are not currently in place, organizations should at least be actively working on them, so we are laying a solid foundation and not *building on sand*. John Kotter's book Leading Change describes a strategy for implementing an organizational transformation, and readers are encouraged to leverage it.

- **Teams in place**, including team Product Owners and Scrum Masters, and are proficient in all basic team practices. If not, address immediately via training.

- **Value Streams Identified** Any required organizational alignment (or re-alignment) has been addressed to ensure good alignment between business and delivery teams. Organization by value streams as opposed to functional silos is critical to ensure solid alignment between the business and delivery organization, and to eliminate handoffs and associated delays or bottlenecks in the flow of information through the organization. The goal is to optimize the system as a whole and not just the delivery processes. The design of both operational (order to cash) and development (concept to release) value streams must be addressed.

- **ARTs identified.** Agile Release Trains support development value streams. ARTs should be designed so that they can release value independently. These trains are typically organized around feature delivery. Where multiple trains are needed to support a large value stream, organize by feature areas, ideally so that each ART can release independently.

- **Teams are cross-functional,** and have all the required skills to deliver valuable, working software. Teams know how to write and produce small slices of valuable functionality as the output of every iteration. Stories meet INVEST criteria and teams deliver *value* via user stories.

- **Continuous Integration and Test Automation** are in place, or in development, so that production-ready software is the output of every iteration. (No separate test phases, no hand-offs, goal is to minimize lead-time from change to production).

Of course, additional roles and practices are required at the program and portfolio levels, we will be discussing these in subsequent chapters.

2. SAFe Portfolio Management

Portfolio Management is the highest-level planning process in the Scaled Agile Framework, and refers to the definition, refinement, prioritization and funding of business initiatives for realization by programs and delivery teams. These initiatives are referred to as *epics* in SAFe, and once approved at the portfolio level, are translated into implementable *features* to be realized by program and delivery teams.

Definitions

Before we start, let's cover some relevant definitions:

- **Project:** A temporary activity to deliver a fixed scope. Typically refers to work of a single team
- **Program**: A collection of linked projects. Involves multiple collaborating teams
- **Portfolio**: A collection of programs, projects or subsidiary portfolios managed as a group to achieve strategic objectives (PMI Definition).
- **Portfolio Management** is the centralized management of one or more portfolios to achieve strategic objectives.

Portfolio Definitions

- Each business unit within an enterprise will have a *portfolio* of revenue-generating products and/or services.
- Each portfolio is guided by a strategy, or set of *Strategic Themes*, and supported by the people and processes required to carry out that strategy.
- Portfolio-level artifacts include: Strategic Themes, Epics (Both Business & Enabler Epics,) a Portfolio Kanban, and a Portfolio Backlog.
- Portfolio Management operates at the front-end of a *Development Value Stream*: The total set of actions required to bring a product or service from concept to launch. SAFe, borrowing from *lean*, distinguishes between 2 types of value stream:

Development Value Stream (Concept-To-Launch): The set of all actions (both value-creating and non-value-creating) required to bring a product or service from concept to launch. Development Value Streams exist to support Operational Value Streams. Development Value Streams are supported by ARTs (Agile Release Trains).

Operational Value Stream (Order-To-Cash): The set of all actions (both value-creating and non-value-creating) required to bring a product or service from order to delivery.

Operational and Development Value Streams

What is an Epic?

Epics represent initiatives for implementing strategy. For example, if an organization selects a strategy of being the lowest cost provider of a product or service, epics might be defined for reducing operational costs of providing that service so that savings can be passed on to consumers. In IT terms, reducing operational expenses might be achieved by automating workflows to eliminate manual processing steps required to provide service or close a sale. In the definition of that epic there should be clear traceability back to the strategic theme that talks about pursuing a strategy of becoming the lowest cost provider or supplier.

What is an Epic?

The term 'epic' can be a frequent source of confusion, particularly in the context of SAFe. In textbook scrum, *epics* are simply large stories, that is, stories that are too big to fit in a single sprint. SAFe however adopts the hierarchy: *Strategic Theme* → *Epic* → *Feature* → *User Story*, where stories fit in iterations, features fit in Program Increments (PI's), and epics require multiple PI's to fully realized in production. In SAFe, epics represent major business initiatives and may require multiple teams and multiple PI's to fully realize. SAFe epics are containers that capture all of the information needed to realize a specific element of the business portfolio. Epics represent initiatives that are of primary importance to the organization. Epics should have a well-defined goal, and hence a finite delivery horizon. The number of epics in progress at any one time should be limited to ensure that available delivery capacity is well-focused. Epics are broken into features which are units of functionality that can be delivered within PI timeboxes. Epics are artifacts of the *problem space* (user needs), whereas features/stories belong in the *solution space* (product features). Epics are defined using a value proposition statement, sometimes captured via Geoffrey Moore's *elevator pitch* format. Features describe how user needs are going to be addressed.

A very useful way of thinking about epics is to separate the problem domain from the solution domain. (This concept has been promoted by Dan Olsen in his book: *The Lean Product Playbook*). Any product, or application, or service that you build exists in the

Solution Space – as do any specifications, feature descriptions, mockups, wire-frames, and so on – the solution space includes the actual product, or any representation of the product. Conversely, descriptions of customer needs belong in the *Problem Space*. Anything that describes the user problem to be solved (Save time, save cost, improve performance, improve accuracy, easier to use, and so on) – these are problems to be solved. For example: *As an insurance underwriter, I would like to reduce the time to produce a quote from 1 hour to under 10 minutes, so that I can be more productive and improve the quality of the policies that I write.* The problem focuses on the *what*, the solution space focuses on the *how*. Epics should be written as *problem descriptions*, whereas features are *solution descriptions*.

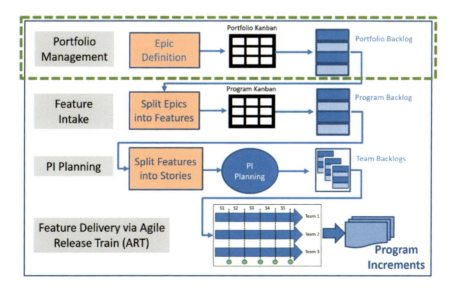

SAFe Portfolio Management in Context

An organization may have more than one portfolio, each addressing unique or different organizational (business, functional or other) strategies, goals and objectives. Large portfolios may contain subsidiary portfolios, usually structured as a hierarchy. For example, portfolios of programs or projects may reside within a larger business-unit portfolio, which, in turn, is nested as one portfolio within the entire enterprise portfolio. Portfolios may also exist at various levels within an organization, such as enterprise, divisional, business unit, or functional.

If a portfolio is a collection of related programs or subsidiary portfolios, then portfolio management refers to the set of practices associated with:

- Portfolio backlog creation, grooming/refinement
- Deciding which initiatives to undertake and in what order
- Frequent adjustment or removing of individual initiatives in the portfolio to ensure ongoing alignment with strategy and objectives.
- Managing the allocation of resources (financial, people, capital assets, intellectual) between portfolio items to deliver business value aligned with organizational strategy.

Portfolio Management Inputs & Outputs

Basic inputs and outputs for portfolio management are as follows:

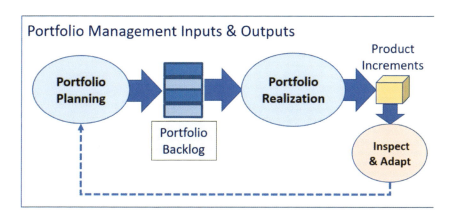

Portfolio Management Inputs and Outputs

Portfolio management is intended to operate as a feedback loop, using *inspect and adapt* to maintain alignment with stakeholders and evolving business conditions. The Portfolio Backlog is a ranked list of business initiatives defined in *epic* format, ready for realization by program delivery teams. The above diagram represents the highest level set of operating practices within an organization that convert business strategy into working products, while adapting continuously and flexibly to the evolving demands of customers and markets.

Creating a Portfolio Backlog

If we expand the input side further into its core elements, we have the following set of activities that ultimately contribute to the construction of a portfolio backlog:

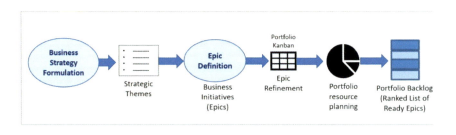

Portfolio Planning and Backlog Construction

The set of basic activities that lead to the creation, refinement and approval of initiatives for the portfolio backlog can be summarized as follows:

- **Business strategy formulation**. This topic is really beyond the scope of the SAFe framework, but the assumption is that someone in the business can articulate a strategy behind any initiatives proposed for implementation. It is highly beneficial for delivery teams to understand the rationale for any features they have been asked to deliver, so they can make the right priority calls and trade-offs. At the highest level of a business, selected strategies might, for example, be one of Michael Porter's four generic

40

competitive strategies, chosen as a result of an analysis of an organization's strengths and weaknesses, weighed against current opportunities and threats in the business environment:

- o Cost Leadership Strategy: Deliver products or services at a lower cost. For example, by automating business procedures, or streamlining existing workflows, a company could pass on some those cost reductions to their customers.
- o Differentiation strategy: Deliver products or services that are differentiated from competitors. Differentiation means the addition of unique features to a product or service that are attractive in the target market.
- o Focus Strategy: Focus on specific market segments. The idea is to identify and create market niches that have not been adequately served by competitors.
- o Innovation Strategy: Develop products or services that offer new and fundamentally different capabilities.

- **Business Epic Creation.** Propose business initiatives designed to realize the strategy. Strategic themes are elaborated into specific initiatives for implementation. These initiatives are defined in *epic* format, with each epic being expressed as a concise

41

statement of value (elevator pitch), and a feature summary that captures the scope of what is needed.

- **Epic Analysis & Refinement**. Epics are analyzed, refined and prioritized to the point that a Go/No-Go business decision can be made, and are well-enough defined that they can be consumed by program teams for PI Planning purposes. At this point at least an outline of the technical solution should be understood, and any technology *enabler epics* identified to support the solution. Analysis will include assigning relative business value and also an estimate of the relative effort to deliver the epic.

- **Epic Ranking & Approval**. Approved epics are added to the portfolio backlog. Epics in the portfolio backlog are ranked taking into account both relative business value and cost of development (for example using Weighted Shortest Job First). Decide which business initiatives make the biggest contributions to strategy and allocate resources accordingly. The Portfolio Backlog is a Unified backlog of business and technology initiatives, objectively ranked using WSJF.

The sequence of activities that takes us from business strategy formulation to approved epics that are ready for consumption by program teams, can be effectively managed by use of a program kanban.

The Portfolio Kanban

SAFe offers a way of defining business epics and of refining them to the point where they can be consumed by program teams. This is accomplished using a Portfolio Kanban to visualize the work, make status explicit, limit work in progress (WIP), and continuously improve the process. Different degrees of epic refinement are reflected in a series of workflow states, each representing more detail than the previous one, until the final state contains those epics that are considered *ready* for consumption by program teams for the creation of product features. Epics that have reached this state are part of the Portfolio Backlog.

The recommended template for an epic includes:

- An epic hypothesis or value statement (elevator-pitch style value statement) – basically, what are we building, who is it for, and why do they need it – See Geoffrey Moore's *Crossing The Chasm* for details and examples.
- A set of core features, or scope definition. It is also helpful spell out what's *not* in scope.
- A Minimum Viable Product (MVP) definition, or what is the minimum feature set for a viable release of this epic.
- A list of any architectural enablers required to support the required features.
- A lightweight business case – some basic economic rationale that the investment is justified.

- A ranking level vs. other epics using WSJF (Weighted Shortest Job First) – See Donald Reinertsen's *Principles of Product Development Flow* for more on WSJF. A simplified example is presented in Chapter 3.

Epics that have achieved the above level of refinement are added to the *portfolio backlog*.

Below is an example of a template for defining an epic. It includes an epic value statement, and a definition of scope:

	Epic Value Statement
For	\<customers\>
Who	\<do something – the "what'\>
Is a	\<solution\>
That	\<provides this value\>
Unlike	\<competitor, current solution, or non-existing solution\>
Our Solution	\<does something better – the "why"\>
	Scope Statement
Features	• Feature 1 • Feature 2 • Feature 3
NFR's	• Non-Functional Requirement 1 • Non-Functional Requirement 2
Out Of Scope	• OOS Feature 1 • OOS Feature 2

Epic Template Example

Spelling out any out-of-scope items is crucial for preserving focus on the essentials, and ensuring effort is not scattered across a wide range of things that may not be of immediate importance.

A portfolio kanban system is an effective way to manage the process of epic refinement and portfolio backlog creation. The portfolio management team drives this process via regular portfolio backlog grooming or refinement meetings. Typical tasks include:

- Create/Review epic definitions
- Review epic business cases
- Identify architectural *enablers*
- Determine priorities, estimates and epic rankings (e.g. using WSJF)
- Update the kanban board so it always accurately reflects the state of the portfolio

Portfolio Kanban Example

Workflow					
Portfolio Planning				Portfolio Realization	
Funnel	Business Review	Solution Analysis	Portfolio Backlog	Implem- enting	Done

All workflow states except *Funnel* are WIP-limited. WIP limits should be set based on the capacity of the next downstream state. WSJF is continuously refined across all kanban states as more details are discovered. The portfolio backlog refinement process should operate on a regular cadence to ensure that progress flows continuously to the program teams.

Portfolio Kanban Workflow States:

- **Funnel** – initial state for all new ideas/proposals pending review and analysis
- **Business Review** – Epic defined in terms of *epic value statement* (elevator pitch-style value statement), with in-scope, out-of-scope items defined (major features). One-page business case available.
- **Solution Analysis** – Solution alternatives reviewed. Technology enablers identified. High-level size estimate, relative ranking (WSJF) vs. other epics, and Go/No-Go decision on moving to the Portfolio Backlog.
- **Portfolio Backlog** (Defined, Estimated, Ranked & Approved Epics).
- **Implementing** – Epics have been elaborated into features and being delivered via Program Increments.
- **Done** – Additional feature development deemed unnecessary.

Portfolio Kanban Operation

- Define a portfolio-level workflow, and be very specific about entry/exit definitions for each state
- Establish a meeting cadence, for example meet weekly, same time/place, invite everyone from the LPM team.
- Portfolio Kanban review is basically a 'stand-up' for purposes of synchronization and alignment (3 questions: what was accomplished, what is being worked on, what is blocked, in terms of progressing epics across the board). Most actual work is done outside the meeting.
- Work the board from Right-to-Left – strive to get epics into Backlog state
- Apply WIP limits to optimize the flow and prevent bottlenecks
- Continuously refine your process to minimize average cycle time per epic from Funnel to Backlog , and from Backlog to Done.

Managing Portfolio Delivery

On the output side of the portfolio management process, each item in the portfolio backlog is brought to life by a delivery *program*, supported by an Agile Release Train (ART), which could be represented as shown in the following diagram where each epic is handled by a separate instance of the SAFe program layer:

48

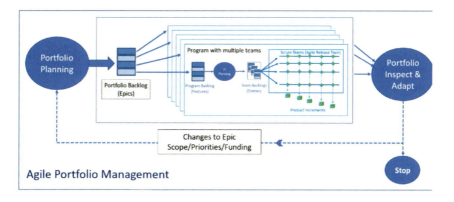

Portfolio *Epics* are elaborated into product or solution features and delivered by an Agile Release Train (ART) via a series of Product Increments. Inspect and Adapt is used as part of the portfolio level feedback loop, which gives an organization the ability to learn and pivot, or make program changes at frequent intervals in order to maintain maximum flexibility (or maximum *business agility*).

The incremental delivery of epics to production is covered in Chapters 3, 4 and 5.

Portfolio Review

All levels of the SAFe framework (Team, Program , Portfolio) are based on inspect & adapt loops based on the PDCA (Plan-Do-Check-Act) cycle, and portfolio management is no exception. At the program level, every PI concludes with a set of

49

formal inspect and adapt activities representing a Pivot Point. The learning from each completed Program Increment can be rolled up into a portfolio-level view of an entire portfolio. This presents opportunities for adjustment or removal of individual initiatives in the portfolio, or for re-balancing investment levels across initiatives to ensure ongoing alignment with overall strategy and objectives.

Data is required to support inspect and adapt at any level of the framework. At the portfolio level data for both in-production and in-development initiatives is required.

A review of the entire portfolio by the portfolio management team should take place on about a once-a-month cadence. Data from both in-development and in-production programs should be reviewed. For in-development programs, data should include a basic program-level burn-up chart, plus a look one level deeper into progress by feature. For in-production programs, revenue trends, customer satisfaction survey data, and quality metrics are the basics that need a review. A well-designed high-level dashboard can give a sense of which programs are being successful and which may need help or adjustments.

Portfolio Management Team Roles

Portfolio management is typically overseen by the senior leadership team in most organizations. These individuals can have various job titles depending on the organization, but specific roles identified by SAFe are:

- **Portfolio Owner**. Final say and approval for priorities, epic ranking, investment allocations for portfolio backlog items.
- **Epic Owners**. Epic definition (business case, value proposition, feature-scope). Responsible for managing epics through the portfolio Kanban system and for securing a Go/No-Go decision on whether to proceed in each case. For those epics that are approved for implementation, the epic owner works with the appropriate program team to ensure epics are elaborated into required features and prioritized appropriately. Epic owners would then provide ongoing consultation and support as epics are evolved through development and into production.
- **Solution Architect**. Solution recommendations. Identification and delivery of architectural runway needed to support epics and associated features.
- **Program Product Owners**. Elaboration of epics into features and management of a program backlog. Planning and delivery of epics via program increments (PI's).

- **LPM – Lean Portfolio Management Team**. The above set of individuals comprise the Portfolio Management Team. This team is engage in both the portfolio backlog creation and portfolio-level reviews to ensure that the overall portfolio is optimally aligned with business strategy and priorities.

Key Portfolio Management Ceremonies

Just like any other level of the SAFe operating framework, it is important to establish a set of portfolio management ceremonies that run on a fixed cadence, and which manage the flow of work through the value stream from strategy definition to working products. The cadence can be adjusted over time to achieve optimum flow.

	Backlog Refinement	Portfolio Planning	Portfolio Review	Process Retro.
What:	Get epics ready for portfolio planning.	Approve, rank and schedule epics.	Review in-development and in-production initiatives, make adjustments	Learn from experience & improve.
When:	Bi-weekly	Quarterly (between PI's)	Monthly	Monthly (following portfolio reviews)
Who:	Portfolio Owner, Epic Owners, Program POs, Architects	Portfolio Owner, Epic Owners, Program POs, Architects, RTE's	Portfolio Owner, Epic Owners, RTE's	Portfolio Owner, Epic Owners, RTE's
How:	Epics well-enough defined to support planning. *Portfolio Kanban* used to manage refinement process.	Epics ranked using objective criteria (ex. WSJF). RTE's provide guidance about when epics can begin.	Epic Owners present data on both in-development and in-production epics. Portfolio Owner decides on adjustments.	Portfolio Owner facilitates. Identify what is working well, needs improving and actions to improve.

Portfolio Management Checklist

- LPM (Lean Portfolio Management) team in place to steer the transformation of business strategy into tangible artifacts (epics) that can be consumed by program teams for implementation.
- Portfolio Kanban system setup to facilitate the analysis and refinement of portfolio epics.
- Portfolio Management operates as a collaboration between Portfolio and Program teams.
- Epics clearly define customer problems in terms of value statements and scope.
- Epics are ranked objectively using WSJF or equivalent method.
- The Portfolio Backlog is a unified business and technical backlog of work (a combination of business epics and architectural enabler epics).
- Cadence established for portfolio management ceremonies (not run on an ad hoc basis).

Once we have a properly defined and prioritized portfolio backlog, program teams can engage to elaborate epics into product features, and from there feed the PI planning process.

3. Constructing A Program Backlog

A program backlog is a ranked list of features targeted for delivery in upcoming program increments or PI's. This backlog is primarily derived from the *Portfolio Backlog*, however features from other sources could be added directly. The amount of time and effort required for a PI planning event will depend entirely on the degree of refinement of this backlog. Backlog construction and the feature refinement process can be managed effectively using a program *kanban*, where different levels of refinement are reflected in a series of workflow states, each showing more detail than the previous one, until the final state contains features that are considered *ready* for PI Planning.

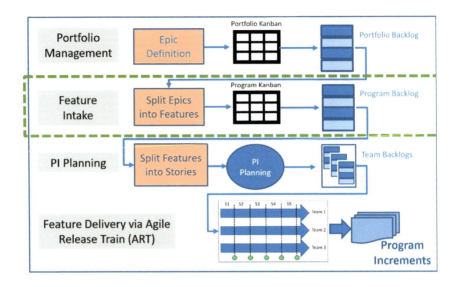

Feature Intake and Program Backlog Construction

Getting to a committed feature set for delivery in a PI is a 2-part process:

- **Feature Intake and Refinement** : output is a *Program Backlog*, that is, a ranked list of ready features representing the objectives for at least the next PI. (Ideally deep enough to supply enough features for at least 1.5 PI's).
- **PI Planning Event** : output is a reconciliation of both dependencies and delivery production capacity to understand how much of the program backlog can be actually committed in the forthcoming PI.

This chapter will focus on the first part of this process.

56

Feature Intake Kanban

SAFe does not prescribe specific states for feature intake and refinement. What follows is one example of how to accomplish this using a kanban.

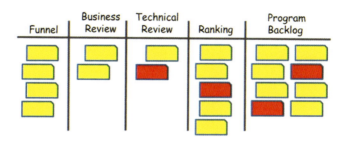

Feature Intake Kanban

The goal is to provide visibility about the state of refinement of any proposed feature. Features that evolve to the program backlog column are considered sufficiently well-defined that delivery teams can create and size user stories. Key states in the intake workflow:

Funnel: Initial placeholder for proposed features. Features may be pulled here from epic definitions in the epic backlog, or directly from other sources. This state is WIP-unlimited.

Business Analysis: Features are reviewed for alignment with strategy, product vision and customer needs, and may be rejected if not considered a good fit. Features are more formally defined with stated benefits and acceptance criteria. Features are given an initial ranking relative to other features in the backlog based on business value and estimated development effort. (Relative ranking, see Chapter 4).

Technical Review: Technical review and analysis by product architects. Outline implementation approach is identified together with any additional 'architectural runway' or 'enabler' items. Feature size estimate is updated based on additional information from technical analysis. Omission or skimping of this step can lead to serious problems in the execution of the PI. Teams needs to be in a position to hit the ground running once the PI commences, and not be required to invest large amounts of time in solving major architectural questions.

Ranking: Feature ranking determined objectively using Weighted Shortest Job First (WSJF) (or other equivalent method). Basically, the numerator (business value) and denominator (feature size or cost estimate) are both estimated relative to all other features in the backlog using Fibonacci. The resulting rank is calculated as the ratio of business value / size (cost).

Program Backlog: Features that have completed all workflow steps, and are fully defined with benefits, acceptance criteria, and architectural dependencies, and have been ranked with respect to all other features planned for the next PI, are considered *Program Backlog* items, and are now ready for user story creation and sizing.

Just as delivery teams continuously refine or 'groom' their iteration backlogs ahead of sprint planning, construction and refinement of a program backlog is intended to be a continuous process (vs. a single big-bang planning event) that is one of the regularly scheduled program-level ceremonies, and should be run at a frequency sufficient to prepare enough ready features for the next PI. The target feature set for the next PI should be in the *ready state* well ahead of the PI planning event to give teams time to digest and understand the new features well enough to break them into user stories and to estimate.

New	Bus. Review	Tech. Review	Rank- ing	Ready
New (Funnel)	**Business Review**	**Technical Review**	**Feature Ranking**	**Ready (Program Backlog)**

• Unrefined Ideas, goals, business objectives	• Items reviewed vs. vision & strategy
	• Features Defined
	  ✓ Benefits
	  ✓ Acceptance Criteria
		• Solution outlined
		• Dependencies
		• Risks
		• Arch. Enablers
		• Gross size estimate
		• Gross effort estimate
			• Features ranked by business value/cost of delay (WSJF)	• Features ready for release planning

Feature Refinement Kanban

This level of feature refinement should be sufficient to support a 2-day PI planning event, where on the first day, features will be elaborated into user stories and sized more accurately. I have worked with some teams who have completed story mapping/story sizing as part of the feature intake process, then requiring only a 1-day PI planning event. (For a 1-day PI planning event, you may want to insert an additional workflow state – Story mapping/sizing – into the Feature Refinement Kanban). The risk with this approach is that program priorities frequently change right up to (and indeed during) a PI Planning event, rendering too much planning ahead of the event a waste.

Note: If you do not have a Kanban tool, just use a spreadsheet:

Feature	New	Bus. Review	Tech. Review	Ranked	Ready
Feature 1	●	●	●	●	●
Feature 2	●	●	●		
Feature 3	●				
Feature 4	●	●	●	●	
Feature 5	●	●			

Feature Intake

The Feature Intake process should operate continuously, say as a weekly event facilitated by a Program-Level Scrum Master (or, *'Release Train Engineer'* (RTE) in SAFe), or 'Chief Product Owner' (or Product Manager). Attendees should include all team PO's and Architects who can contribute to moving feature requests across the Kanban board by contributing increasing amounts of detail about each feature. The goal is to have at ideally 1.5 PI's worth of ready features available at least 2-4 weeks ahead of the next PI Planning event.

Feature Intake Kanban Operation:

- Define a Feature Intake workflow. Be explicit about entry/exit criteria for each state.
- Cadence: Meet weekly, same time/place, with everyone on the below 'Who' list. Experiment with this cadence to ensure 1.5 PI's worth of ready features available in Program Backlog at least 3 weeks out from the PI Planning event.
- Who Attends: Product Managers, System Architects, RTE, Epic Owners.
- Work the board from Right-to-Left – strive to get features into Backlog state.
- Can be facilitated by an RTE, or Product Manager.
- Apply WIP limits to optimize the flow, and prevent bottlenecks.
- Intake meeting is basically a 'stand-up'. Most work is done outside the meeting
- Continuously refine the process to minimize average cycle time per feature from Funnel to Backlog

Feature Intake Kanban Operation

Feature Intake Roles and Responsibilities

Product Manager – Owns the Program Backlog and works with Release Trains and Epic Owners to establish objectives for Program Increments.

System Architect – Responsible for defining outline technical approach for individual features, and for definition and delivery of architectural runway extensions or enabler features to support the solution.

Epic Owner(s) – Owners of items in the Portfolio Backlog, from which much of the program backlog is derived. Epic Owners help marshal portfolio items through feature definition and delivery.

Release Train Engineer (RTE) – Facilitates all of the program-level ceremonies, including PI Planning and Scrum-Of-Scrums.

Ranking Features With WSJF

It is important that features in the program backlog are properly and objectively ranked for delivery. WSJF – Weighted Shortest Job First provides a mechanism for doing this. Here is a somewhat simplified method for doing this:

1. Get proposed feature list
2. Assign "business value points" to each feature using a Fibonacci scale – just relative ranking. Use Planning Poker, this is a team exercise with PO's, Architects, and other contributors. Complete this step for entire feature list before moving on to step 3.
3. Assign "cost points" (or "size points", or "Feature Points"). Again, relative sizing using a Fibonacci scale.
4. Rank = Value/Cost. (This is WSJF slightly simplified). Sets priorities for release planning.

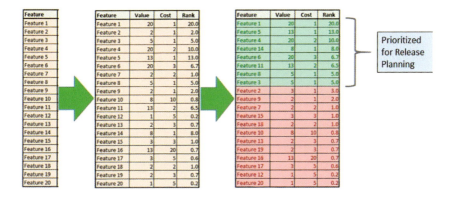

Ranking Features With WSJF

Feature Definition Template

Features that have made it all the way to the Ready (Backlog) state, should have the following information:

```
Feature Name:
----------------------------------
Benefits:
•      ----------------------------
•      ----------------------------
Acceptance Criteria:
•      ----------------------------
•      ----------------------------
•      ----------------------------
Architectural Runway Needs:
•      ----------------------------
•      ----------------------------
```

Feature Definition Template

Benefits. Spelling out benefits helps ensure that delivery teams understand the actual value is being provided to the user. For example, for a smartphone feature, 'Favorites':

- Feature: Favorites is a list of contacts that are called frequently.
- Benefit: Makes it unnecessary for a user to search through a long list of contacts, making the process faster and more convenient.

Acceptance Criteria. Acceptance criteria are recommended for all levels of requirements (epics, features, stories). They should provide an unambiguous definition of expected behavior of the feature, and also serve to delineate the scope boundary of what is required or not required. Both functional and non-functional (e.g. performance) requirements should be defined.

Architectural Runway Needs. It is important to spell out any architectural or technical infrastructure prerequisites required to support the feature. This also acts as a check to confirm that these topics have been reviewed and agreed to as part of the feature refinement process.

Feature Intake Process Checklist

- A Feature Intake Kanban system has been setup, and supports the definition, analysis, and readiness of features for addition to the Program Backlog.
- Architects are engaged throughout the intake process to ensure additional architectural runway and any required technical enablers are defined.
- Program Backlog features have been ranked using WSJF.
- A feature intake cadence has been established such that the program backlog is ready and socialized with product owners at least 3 weeks prior to the PI planning event.

With a program backlog comprising a ranked list of ready features, we are now ready for PI Planning.

4. The PI Planning Event

Introduction

In the last chapter we covered how to construct a program backlog, a fundamental prerequisite step for the PI Planning process. In this chapter we will walk through each of the steps required to achieve the goals of PI Planning.

PI Planning Goals

The primary purpose of PI Planning is to gain alignment between business stakeholders and program teams on a common set of Program Objectives and Team Objectives for the next PI time-box. There are in fact 2 specific sets of deliverables from the event: a feature delivery timeline by team, and a list of program objectives scored by business value.

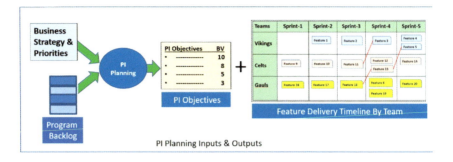

PI Planning Inputs & Outputs

PI Planning Event Inputs and Outputs

The above chart summarizes what we are attempting to achieve during a PI Planning event. One primary input to the process, the Program Backlog, as discussed in the last chapter, should be sufficiently refined to support user story creation and estimation. The better the degree of refinement of this backlog the more accurate will be the PI scope estimation and the feature delivery timeline. The other major input to the process is the articulation of business strategy and business priorities by the business stakeholders. These provide a framework for the teams to make tradeoffs in planning with the goal of ensuring that maximum business value is delivered, and for achieving the highest possible degree of alignment between delivery teams and stakeholders.

The process flow for going from inputs to outputs can summarized as follows:

PI Planning Process Flow:

- Prework: Program Backlog Construction & Refinement
  - Portfolio epics elaborated into features
  - Features sufficiently refined to support creation and sizing of user stories
- PI Scope Estimation
  - Features mapped into user stories
  - Stories estimated in points or capacity units
  - Stories scheduled into iterations
  - Maximum scope of PI determined
- Feature Delivery Timeline
  - Feature delivery schedule estimated to nearest iteration
- PI Business Objectives
  - Teams confirm which business goals are being addressed (fully or partially) by feature deliverables
  - Stakeholders score objectives based on perceived business value
- Teams & Stakeholders Confirm Alignment on Scope & Objectives
  - Program risks are assessed
  - Confidence vote from teams and stakeholders

PI Planning is typically carried out in a 2-day event, with everyone participating in person including business stakeholders, program management and all delivery teams. The general outline of the 2 days is as follows:

PI Planning Day 1: Teams create draft plans

- Introductions & Agenda Review
- Business Context: Vision, Strategy & Roadmap
- Architecture Updates
- Team Breakouts #1
  1. Story Mapping (create stories from features)
  2. Story Sizing
  3. Story & Feature Scheduling
  4. Draft PI Objectives
- Teams present draft plans with risks & impediments
- Leadership review & problem solving

PI Planning Day 2: Finalize plans & confidence vote

- Planning Adjustments from leadership team
- Team Breakouts #2:
  1. Team plan adjustments
  2. Updated Feature Scheduling
  3. Updated Objectives
  4. Risks ROAM'ed
- Stakeholder plan reviews and objectives scoring
- Program wall-board finalized
- Program Risk Review
- Program Confidence Vote
- PI Planning Event Retrospective

PI Planning Event Outline Agenda and Process Flow

Day 1 - Draft Plans

Creating User Stories from Features

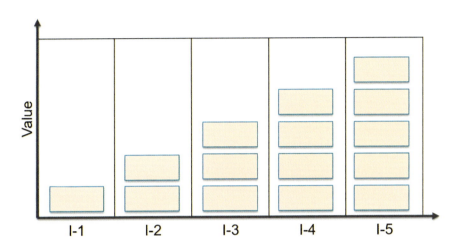

Value Delivery Via User Stories

In the first team breakout session, each team decomposes their features into user stories. User stories are small pieces of functionality that can be developed, tested and demonstrated in a single iteration, while still representing something of value to a user. Story writing can be a challenge for many teams, and this practice may take a considerable time to master. Of the 12 principles behind the Agile Manifesto, 2 are especially relevant here:

- Our highest priority is to satisfy the customer through early and continuous delivery of working software
- Working software is the primary measure of progress.

71

A good definition of *done* for a user story should include everything necessary to make the story production-ready. If we hold to that, then the output of every iteration is a production-quality increment of the product that provides value to actual users. Of course, programs are unlikely to push individual user stories to production, and multiple stories, or even multiple features, may be necessary to produce a minimum viable product (MVP) that is worth shipping. However, it is important to have incremental working software as the output of every iteration so that stakeholders can assess business value and provide critical feedback. User Stories are a concept that make it possible to deliver on the fundamental agile value proposition of continuous value delivery, illustrated in the above diagram.

There are many ways to tackle the problem of breaking features into pieces that are both *small* and *valuable*. One approach we will touch upon is the technique of Story Mapping. Basic story mapping is summarized in the following diagram using a simple e-commerce application as an example:

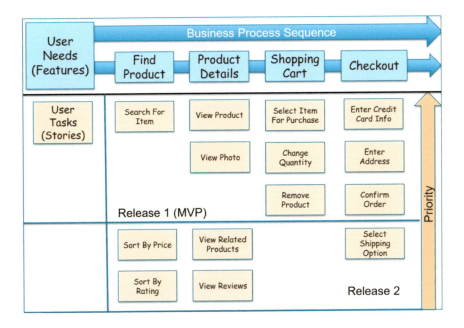

Basic Story Mapping

In story mapping, we talk about the *backbone* of the application, basic core functions needed to provide the capabilities that a user needs. We then build out the *skeleton*, by adding those items that define the individual tasks a user needs to carry out within each function. The three basic sets of steps involved are as follows:

1. Create the "backbone" of the story map. These are the large activities (features) that the users must do to carry out the overall solution or application. Capture the end-to-end user experience. Start by asking "what do users do?" Layout the backbone and skeleton framework on a

73

wall, and use a team brainstorming approach to get core features identified quickly. In the above example the backbone comprises 4 basic functions: *Search* for products, *Review* product details, add product to *Shopping Cart*, and finally *Checkout*.

2. Then start adding steps that happen within each backbone item – call these the "skeleton". Ask, what are the specific things a user would do to accomplish the goal described by the feature. For example what are the elements or sub-functions of *Search*. These activities may be considered user stories. (They may need to be split into even smaller items later so they fit in a single iteration). Arrange the stories in priority order.

3. Create the Minimum Viable Product - "MVP". This is where you select a set of user stories or options that can give you the minimum acceptable end-to end user experience.

We do not need fully defined stories at this point – i.e. meeting a definition of *ready*, just story titles that describe the purpose of the story. These stories can be elaborated to meet a full definition of ready, later in backlog refinement sessions. The reason for this is practical. A team with a velocity of say, 50 story points, may need to create 50 – 60 stories (A dozen 3-5 point stories per iteration times 5 iterations for the PI). Refinement sessions normally take around 2 hours per 2-week sprint. In PI Planning, teams will need to create and estimate roughly 5 sprints worth of stories in a 3-hour breakout session. Hence it is simply not possible to produce 5 sprints worth of stories meeting a definition of ready in the allotted time. It is important to get the stories identified quickly so that the total scope of the PI can be understood.

Just as teams will not have the time to produce large numbers of iteration-ready user stories in a single 3-hour breakout session, they will also not have the time to perform a Planning Poker exercise for each of those stories, and thus a simpler approach will be needed.

One approach for quickly estimating a large number of stories is 'Affinity Estimation', a team-based exercise where stories are written on post-its and arranged on a board in groups or columns based on relative size. Use T-shirt sizes or story points to group stories – this is a relative sizing exercise only -i.e. an 8-point story is as big as a 5-point and a 3-point story combined. The goal is to achieve a reasonable consensus within the team. The basic idea is that estimation errors will be distributed fairly evenly between too large and too small, and should average out overall. Teams should easily be able to size 50-60 stories in under an hour. Story estimates can be fine-tuned later using Planning Poker, as part of the regular backlog refinement sessions within the PI.

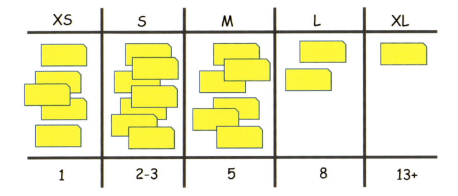

Affinity Estimation

For teams with no experience with story-pointing, or no established velocity, a capacity-based estimation approach can also be used. Though do not attempt to estimate to a granularity of less than a day, and of course, strive to keep all stories smaller than a maximum of 5 days of effort. Also, do not attempt to estimate by breaking stories into implementation tasks. This is simply not feasible in the time available. Whatever approach is used, we will need this data later in planning to estimate the maximum scope that can be delivered in the PI. The official SAFe recommended estimation approach for new teams is as follows.

SAFe Capacity-Based Planning:

- Give every full-time developer and tester on the team 8 points (assuming a 2-week iteration). Thus, assume only 80% of capacity is available for productive work. Basically 1 point per day per person, up to 80% of available capacity in a 10-day iteration.
- Subtract 1 point for every vacation day and holiday
- Select a small story that would take roughly half a day to code and test. Call it a 1-point story.
- Estimate all other stories relative to that one.

SAFe Capacity-Based Estimation

In SAFe, 1 day of development/test effort is equivalent to 1 point. This is not an unreasonable place to start (though agile purists will strongly object!). This approach ensures that we can produce estimates even in the absence of an established team velocity. (This also provides a way to normalize estimates across all teams in a release train. Thus, as well as knowing individual team velocities, we also have knowledge of train capacity/velocity. At the portfolio planning level, we might want to know how much train capacity we will have available over the next number of PI's).

Whatever approach is used, when the exercise is complete we will have an estimate for all user stories, and combining that data with knowledge of team velocities, or team capacities, we should be able to determine of how much of the program backlog can be achieved in the next PI time-box .

Each team participating in the PI Planning event should have their own team wall-board set up in the team planning area, and these should look something like the example below. Each team wall board should comprise: One flip-chart page per iteration on which stories are displayed and reconciled with team velocity or capacity. Additionally there should be one page to capture risks to the team's deliverables, and another page to list the team's PI Objectives. In this step of the planning process, each team will allocate their stories to individual sprints in the PI. The allocation is done taking into account story size and team velocity or capacity. Do not overcommit the amount work planned for each sprint. Sprints should be loaded to about 80% of capacity/velocity to allow for unforeseen changes or newly discovered work items. Also, story scheduling within sprints should be done in a way to try and complete one entire feature before starting a new one, that is, avoid having multiple features in progress at the same time throughout the PI.

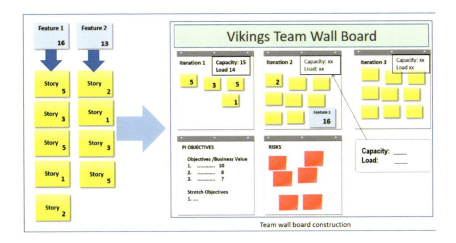

Team wall board construction

Team Wall Board

This step consists of transferring the stories identified in the Story Mapping step to the Team Wall Board, taking into account story sizes and sprint velocities or capacities. When this exercise has been completed, each team should be able to determine in which iteration each of their *features* will be completed. Teams may of course need to synchronize with other teams on feature completion where multiple teams are involved in delivery of individual features, and where dependencies must be accounted for. How each team determines how much scope can be delivered is summarized in the following section.

Once teams have an idea of which iteration each of their features will be completed in, the Program Wall Board should also be updated. This will provide program and leadership teams with an overall summary of initial planning results, and help to highlight any major dependencies or problems that need to be addressed.

PI Scope Estimation

Once we have estimates for all the stories within a feature, we can then estimate the size of the overall feature which is simply the sum of the story estimates. We continue this process until we have estimates for all requested features for the PI. Estimating the achievable scope for the PI is now a matter of reconciling feature estimates with velocity or capacity. This is be done on a team-by-team basis. Below is an example to illustrate the process.

Let's assume the following situation for an individual team:

- Project start: Jan 01
- Project finish: March 12
- Duration: 10 weeks
- Iterations: 5 (10/2)
- Team actual velocity: 50 (points per iteration)
- Maximum deliverable points: 250 (5 X 50)
- Make Scope/Schedule tradeoffs based on business priorities.

Let's assume that this team considered a set of 12 features for the PI, and the results of their story and feature sizing exercise came out as follows:

Team feature size estimates:

Rank	FR#	Feature	Status	Points
1	FR-1001	Feature One	Defined	18
2	FR-1002	Feature Two	Defined	17
3	FR-1003	Feature Three	Defined	15
4	FR-1004	Feature Four	Defined	32
5	FR-1005	Feature Five	Defined	30
6	FR-1006	Feature Six	Defined	38
7	FR-1007	Feature Seven	Defined	20
8	FR-1008	Feature Eight	Defined	15
9	FR-1009	Feature Nine	Defined	36
10	FR-1010	Feature Ten	Defined	28
11	FR-1011	Feature Eleven	Defined	27
12	FR-1012	Feature Twelve	Defined	33

249 pts (Rank 1 through 10)

309 pts (Rank 1 through 12)

Since the team has a total velocity/capacity of 250, it seems that they are only in a position to deliver features 1 through 10, not all 12 features. This fact would be recognized as a significant risk and reflected as such on their risk chart. At the leadership problem solving session at the end of the first day a decision would need to be made to either accept that only the first 10 features are in scope, or to perform de-scoping within individual features to try and get all 12 back in scope, or, to re-allocate staff from other parts of the release train to help address the capacity shortfall. Whatever approach might be taken it is very much a data-driven decision.

When all teams have completed this exercise we should have enough data to populate the program wall board. This can be done at this step, or after the leadership planning updates on the following day.

Setting Team PI Objectives

Each team prepares a list of objectives for the PI, stated in business language. The goal here is not for the delivery teams to inform the stakeholders what the business objectives of the PI are. The purpose of this exercise is to confirm alignment on how well the planned feature deliverables address the business strategy and priorities presented at the beginning of the PI Planning event, and which are to a large extent represented in the epic definitions from which most of the program backlog is derived.

Team PI Objectives are more than just a list of their feature deliverables. Some features may be reflected in highly technical language and it may not be obvious to a business stakeholder how they contribute to business initiatives or strategy. Some business objectives may require multiple features for their achievement. PI Objectives may be a combination of planned features written in business language, or, a high-level distillation of multiple features into a smaller number of key objectives. In some cases, objectives might require collaboration between multiple teams. They might also include 'enabler' features, or even major refactoring or technical debt reduction activities. Thus the purpose of this exercise is to summarize the work of the delivery teams into business or user-facing language, so that the degree of alignment between team deliverables and business strategy can be assessed. Think of objectives as problems to be solved or opportunities to be pursued for the user. Think of features as the solutions to those problems and opportunities.

PI objectives should be SMART: Specific, Measurable, Achievable, Realistic, Time-Bound. This is because at the end of each PI, the program holds an Inspect & Adapt event where teams will demonstrate these objectives to stakeholders and receive quantitative feedback on how well objectives were met.

The PI Objective scoring exercise will take place once the team plans are finalized on day 2 of the event.

Team Risk Assessments

Throughout the PI Planning exercise, teams should also be maintaining a list of risks or impediments that they see potentially impacting their objectives. Add these risks to the team wall-board for transparency and visibility. In particular, teams should be prepared to discuss risks they need help with from outside the team.

The End of The Iron Triangle:

In the old days, release planning was a 3-way debate about scope, schedule and quality. If we operate under the principle that quality is a given, that is, built into the work produced in each iteration via definitions of *done* and supporting XP practices, and that the schedule is also fixed by operating within a standardized delivery time-box, then the only remaining variable to be estimated is scope. This is the primary purpose of the PI Planning event. At fixed intervals, usually every 12 weeks, the organization produces a production-quality, potentially deployable product increment. Organizations may elect not to deploy every one of these releases, or as the saying goes, produce on cadence, deliver on demand. Deployment becomes a business decision, separate from any development considerations. The quality of all PI's is completely consistent, assuming the investment has been made to put all the prerequisite practices in place.

Draft Plan Presentations

Once teams have completed their draft plans during their breakout sessions (including stories and features by sprint, team PI objectives and risks), each team presents their plans to the entire gathering, stakeholders and other teams. Teams will need to highlight if the requested scope cannot be met due to capacity or specific risks that they have identified. A team confidence vote at this point is optional, but may be deferred until plans are finalized on the following day.

Leadership Review And Problem Solving

Before Day 1 wraps up, the leadership team will review the proposed plans and overall draft program plan, and discuss any major problems or disconnects. Adjustments may need to be made to the PI goals and /or feature priorities in order to achieve maximum possible business value from the PI. Once teams have produced their estimates it may become clear to the leadership team that the value being delivered in some areas does not justify the required level of investment, and that some rethinking of priorities is warranted. This may translate into de-scoping of some work, or of re-positioning of teams to reflect revised business priorities. The leadership team must be prepared to announce any changes at the beginning of the next session on the following day.

Day 2 - Finalizing Plans

The layout of the second day is generally as follows:

- Updates from leadership team on any adjustments to the program
- Second breakout sessions for all teams to update plans (changes to scope, delivery schedule, PI Objectives and risks)
- Teams update Program Wallboard
- Teams present updated plans (feature timeline, PI objectives, risks).
- Team PI objectives scored by stakeholders
- Team confidence votes
- Program confidence vote
- Event retrospective

Planning Updates

Day 2 kicks off with a readout from the leadership team to address any needed changes in program scope or priorities. Teams then breakout again to make adjustments to sprints, feature delivery dates, team PI Objectives and risks. Team wall boards are again used to manage this process.

Consolidated Program Wall Board

Once teams have arrived at close to the final versions of their plans, the Program Wall Board should be updated. This should ideally happen before the updated plan presentations, and the team should walk through their feature delivery timeline as part of their presentation. To recap, at this point all teams should have made the following planning progress:

- Features broken into small user stories
- Stories estimated in story points (or in capacity units)
- Stories allocated to iterations, and feature completion dates understood to nearest iteration.

Teams	Sprint-1	Sprint-2	Sprint-3	Sprint-4	Sprint-5
Vikings		Feature 1	Feature 2	Feature 3	Feature 4 / Feature 5
Celts	Feature 9	Feature 10	Feature 11	Feature 12 / Feature 13	Feature 14
Gauls	Feature 16	Feature 17	Enabler 1	Feature 6 / Feature 19	Feature 20

Program Wall Board

In the above example, Team Vikings has 5 features targeted for delivery in the PI, with Feature 1 estimated for completion in Sprint 2, Feature 2 in Sprint 3 and so on. We see that Feature 3 has a

90

dependency on Feature 11 from the Celts team. This is indicated by a piece of colored yarn connecting both features on the board.

The program wall-board shows the consolidated feature completion timeline by team. Do not put user stories on the program board – show features only. Also show any technology enablers, and indicate any other major events like major demos or other significant milestones. Dependencies either with other teams or with teams outside the train should be shown and indicated with yarn.

The Program Wall Board

Many teams, new to PI Planning, are frequently confused about the purpose of the Program Wall Board. So it is worth emphasizing some key points about this important artifact.

- Displays the feature delivery timeline per team – which iteration each feature gets delivered in.
- Shows other major milestones occurring within the program such as release dates or other major events.
- Shows dependencies between features or between features and enabler items. These dependencies are shown by connecting the items with colored string.
- Represents the plan of record of how much of the program backlog will be delivered in the forthcoming PI timebox.
- Used as a reference for Scrum-Of-Scrums or ART-Sync meetings during PI execution.
- Not used to track individual user stories

The Program Wall Board

Scoring PI Objectives

Teams will present their updated PI Objectives as part of their final plan updates. Business stakeholders will circulate, team by team, to review these objectives with the team and score them, assigning a 'business value' between 0-10, where 10 represents the highest business value. The most valuable PI Objective for any team would be given a score of '10', then all remaining PI Objectives are scored relative to that first 10. BV can either scored as relative within the team, or relative to the overall train. Business stakeholders are likely to challenge teams where objectives are not clear or demonstrable, or do not meet at least some of the SMART criteria. We want to see objectives defined in such a way that they can be demonstrated at the Inspect & Adapt at the end of the PI, and that the actual value delivered can be assessed in an objective way.

Before the planning event for the next PI, time is scheduled to demonstrate the accomplishments of each team. Business stakeholders will rate the original objectives based on what has been actually achieved – this data is the basis of the Program Predictability Metric. (Pass out a printed list of PI objectives with original rankings to the stakeholders with additional an column for actuals).

PI Objectives BV	Stretch Objectives
• ------------------- 10 • ------------------- 8 • ------------------- 5 • ------------------- 3 • ------------------- 1	• Use for low confidence or high-risk objectives • Do not count in velocity/capacity • Not part of team commitment

PI Objectives

Final Plan Reviews

Each team's planning outputs are collected to the front of the room for presentation. Teams present their plans (Feature delivery timeline, scored PI objectives) to the entire PI Planning event attendees for discussion and feedback.

During PI planning each team identifies risks or impediments to meeting their PI objectives. Anything that may impact a team's ability to meet an objective is considered a risk. Risks are reviewed in front of all teams/stakeholders and *ROAM'ed* – that is, assigned to 1 of 4 categories:

- **Resolved**: the risk is no longer a concern.
- **Owned**: risk is unresolved but now has an owner who will work to resolve it.
- **Accepted**: risk accepted as a 'fact of life', and team will live with it.
- **Mitigated**: partial solution or workaround identified to lessen the impact.

Risk ROAMing

Team Confidence Vote

Following each team's risk review, a team confidence vote is taken. A simple 'fist of five' vote is taken from the entire team, where 1=No Confidence, and 5 = Very High Confidence. Any vote with 2 fingers or less will need to be heard, and the ensuing discussion may result in additional actions or adjustments to the plan.

Program Risk Review

Those risks that the teams have ROAM'd, and have been unable resolve or mitigate should be brought to the front of the room and added to program risk list. These risks are then also ROAM'd, with the program team, and results considered as part of the final program confidence vote.

Program Confidence Vote

Once all teams have presented their plans, and the program risk review has been completed, a program confidence vote will be taken using the same 'fist of five' technique. This is to gauge the confidence level of the overall program – stakeholders and delivery teams. Each person attending the event responds by holding up the number of fingers that corresponds to the level of support in meeting the program objectives. If any individual holds up fewer than three fingers, he/she is given the opportunity to state their objections or concerns. Any outstanding risks or concerns may need more time allocated to attempt to get to a resolution or at least a mitigation.

The goal for the confidence vote is not to get every event participant in full agreement with all of the objectives and associated risk assessment. That is unlikely to ever happen considering one might have up to a dozen delivery teams, plus a large group of business and organizational leaders, with a broad range of interests and priorities. The goal is consensus, which we will define as reaching a level of agreement that says "this is a plan that I think will work and that I can support". The Five Finger Consensus (or Fist of Five) technique is effective at quickly getting a large group to agreement, without compromising the overall quality of the solution, with strong, but not necessarily unanimous support.

Five Finger Consensus

Event Retrospective

Before the final wrap up, the RTE facilitates a brief retrospective on the PI planning event, so that improvements can be made for the next time. The process used should be kept as simple as possible, typically:

- Sticky notes used to capture comments on: what went well, what did not go well, and suggested improvements.
- Dot Voting used to prioritize the comments and issues.
- Actions agreed for improvements for next PI.

PI Objectives Rollup and Event Close

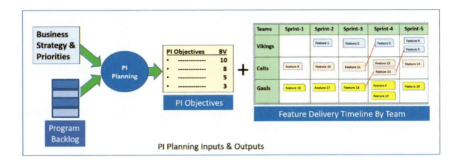

Major Event Artifacts: PI Objectives & Feature Delivery Timeline

Once the event is closed, the RTE and other program stakeholders collect all of the individual team objectives and compile an overall set of program objectives. The overall program objectives are used to communicate externally beyond the program team. The program wall board should also be preserved – either physically or electronically or both. The 2 primary artifacts of the event – PI Objectives List and Program Wall Board – can be put to excellent use for the program Scrum-of-Scrums as progress is made through the PI execution.

PI Planning Process Summary

We have just walked through a process that takes us from a ranked list of features (program backlog) as input, to a comprehensive and agreed-to plan which includes feature delivery scope, feature delivery timeline and business objectives.

99

This is accomplished over a 2-day event using the following sequence of steps:

1. Pre-Work: Feature Intake and Refinement (Program Backlog)
2. Story Mapping
3. Story Sizing
4. Story & Feature Scheduling
5. PI Objectives Setting
6. Risk list compilation
7. Team Draft Plan Reviews
8. Leadership Review & Problem Solving
9. Program Adjustments from Leadership
10. Team Plan Adjustments
11. Program Wall Board Update
12. Plan Reviews and Objectives Scoring
13. Team Confidence Votes
14. Program Confidence Vote
15. PI Planning Event Retrospective
16. Event Close and Wrap-Up

PI Planning Process Steps Summary

Teams leave the event with plans for each of the 5 iterations that make up the next PI, plus a set of business objectives agreed to and ranked by stakeholders. These plans will of course be refined and adjusted over the course of the next PI, but should serve as a very solid baseline plan.

In the next chapter we will look at how we track the program and make adjustments where necessary to ensure that the most important objectives are achieved.

5. PI Execution Practices

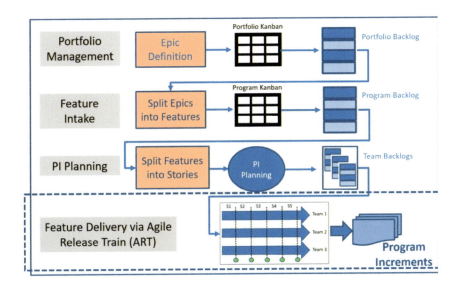

Feature Delivery Via Agile Release Trains

The program level is where each of the pieces built by individual delivery treams are assembled into a working system. A primary goal here is to optimize the interactions between teams. This is accomplished via a set of routine feedback loops: stand-ups, demos, and retros. The program board is an essential tool to help make dependencies between teams visible, and then to manage them. A SAFe program loop operates in many ways like a scaled-up version of scrum. SAFe's program-level practices serve the same purpose as those at the iteration level, except that they are focused on maximizing the value output from an entire ART. Like scrum, a SAFe program increment is intended to run as a PDCA cycle, with its own Inspect and Adapt activities, where the plan, the product and the process used to develop it are continuously reviewed and improved. We are all familiar with diagrams like the following depicting scrum:

The Scrum Framework

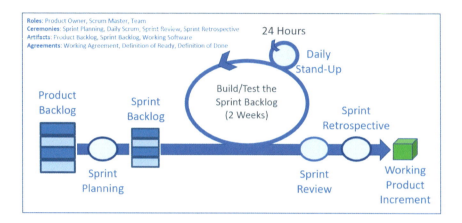

Though not typically represented like this in the SAFe literature, the following diagram provides an equivalent perspective of the SAFe program-level framework as a Plan-Do-Check-Adjust cycle:

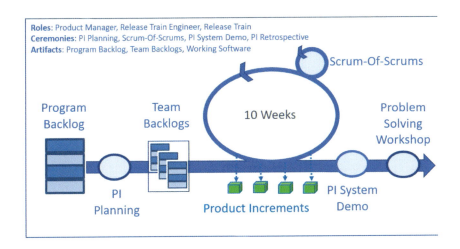

Roles: Product Manager, Release Train Engineer, Release Train
Ceremonies: PI Planning, Scrum-Of-Scrums, PI System Demo, PI Retrospective
Artifacts: Program Backlog, Team Backlogs, Working Software

SAFe Program Framework

Program-level inspect and adapt practices compared with scrum/team-level practices might be summarized as follows:

	Team	Program
Planning	Sprint Planning	PI Planning
I&A The Plan	Daily Standup	Scrum-Of-Scrums
I&A The Product	Sprint Review	System Demos
I&A The Process	Sprint Retrospective	Problem Solving Workshop

Team vs. Program PDCA Cycles

Program Synchronization

Beyond the individual team-level practices like scrum, Kanban, or XP, additional practices are required to keep all teams within the program synchronized. Including:

105

- All teams operate on a synchronized cadence – iterations are the same length (2 weeks) and start and finish on the same day.
- Common definition of *done* (feature and story. Teams still have their own team-specific parts.
- Cross-team working agreement(s). In addition to team working agreement, how will teams interact? (How often will they meet, what will be discussed, how will problems be resolved?).
- Cross-team Demo / Review
- Program Stand-Up Meeting (aka Scrum-Of-Scrums, or 'ART Sync'.)

Team synchronization is necessary to optimize the interaction between teams and manage dependencies, so that teams can produce and demonstrate fully integrated working software at the end of each iteration, as illustrated in the following diagram:

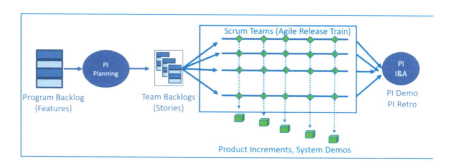

ART Synchronization

Scrum of Scrums (ART Sync)

Scrum teams are very familiar with the *daily stand-up,* where on a daily basis, the team checks their progress against the sprint goal, and makes any adjustments necessary to stay on track. Think of this as a mini-PDCA (*Plan-Do-Check-Adjust*) cycle that runs with a frequency of 24-hours.. Because this is done on a daily basis it eliminates the necessity of communication via status reports, enabling a fast response to emerging problems or opportunities.

The Scrum-of-scrums is a part of the program-level PDCA cycle. That is, it's a regular opportunity for the program team to *check* on the progress of the program and to make *adjustments* in response to any emerging problems, opportunities or changing business priorities.

Inputs: Sufficient data to confirm program is on- or off-track for achieving its objectives. At minimum, the program board constructed during PI planning, plus list of program objectives (guidance for any changes that might be required). The program board shows the feature delivery timeline by team. This board may need to be updated at the end of each iteration to reflect any new realities. One might also maintain a program level Kanban showing the progress of each feature through its workflow – example below:

Teams	To Do	In Dev	System Test	Ready for PO Appr.	Ready For Prod.
Vikings	Feature 1	Feature 2		Feature 5	
Celts	Feature 9 / Feature 10	Feature 11	Feature 12 / Feature 13		Feature 14
Gauls	Feature 16 / Feature 17	Enabler 1	Feature 6	Feature 19	Feature 20

Feature Status Tracking Board

Each workflow state needs to be defined so there is no ambiguity about the status of each feature. For example:

To Do	In Progress	Pending Approval	Done
To Do: Column is for features planned at recent PI Planning event. Features remain in this column until at least one story is started. Program PO manages this column. **In Progress**: Features in this state when at least 1 story is in progress. This column can be split into separate states for Dev. And Test if desired. **Pending PO Approval**: Feature is ready to be demo'd & moved to done. Program PO will determine when feature is complete enough to move to Done state. **Done**: Feature is done/complete. Done is based on a shared understanding between the Epic Owner, Program PO, and relevant team PO's. Shared understanding topics might include: remaining work/stories, NFRs, quality, action plans.			

Scrum-Of-Scrums Mechanics: Regularly scheduled meeting, facilitated by a program scrum master (RTE in SAFe) with representatives ('ambassadors') from each team. Discuss what features are planned for delivery this sprint, any related dependencies, and any problems or impediments that need to be addressed. Program-level impediments are things that are beyond the control of individual teams to resolve and may have program-wide impact. A program impediment list should be maintained by the RTE and either resolved or escalated further if necessary. Whereas team-level standups are focused on sprint goals, the scrum-of-scrums should be about PI goals. Remember that one of the outputs of the PI planning event is a ranked list of program objectives. Things can and do change on a program mid-flight, and the scrum-of-scrums needs to be monitoring the overall health of the program and making adjustments for the purpose of ensuring maximum value delivery. If any single objective fails to be realized, the goal is to maximize the overall success of the program, not of any one individual team.

One way to operate the meeting is to cycle through each team asking program-level versions of the *3 questions:*

- What has my team accomplished towards its PI objectives since the last time we met
- Which PI goal is my team working on completing next, and
- What impediments does my team currently have that may impact the program?

Outputs:

- Updated program radiator (program wall board, and release burn-up chart).
- Actions or plan adjustments to address problems or other required changes
- Aligned program team (ART)

Measuring Program Progress

The program burn-up chart is another useful information radiator. This chart shows overall completed story points per iteration, and can be used to identify early signs of risk. For additional detail, a feature-level completion chart can be constructed, which can show progress at the level of individual features.

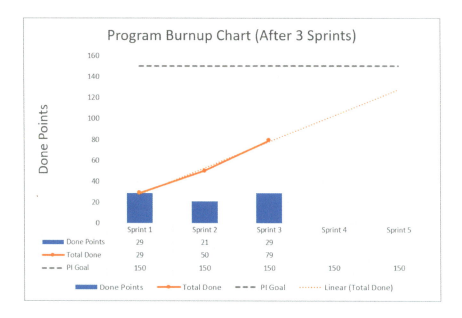

	Sprint 1	Sprint 2	Sprint 3	Sprint 4	Sprint 5
Done Points	29	21	29		
Total Done	29	50	79		
PI Goal	150	150	150	150	150

PI Burn-up Chart

The program burn-up chart can be constructed by taking a snapshot of the feature progress dataset below at the end of each iteration.

At the next level of detail, a feature completion chart gives a useful view of progress at the individual feature level. There are many ways to draw a feature completion chart, for example:

112

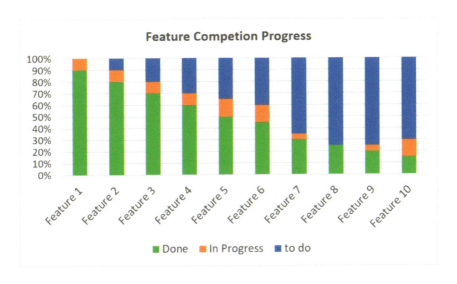

Progress By Feature Chart

The above chart shows percent done vs. percent in progress vs. percent to-do by feature. This data could be based on story points or simply story counts. An alternative (more scalable) way to present such data could be as follows - X-axis is story points or a simple story count per feature:

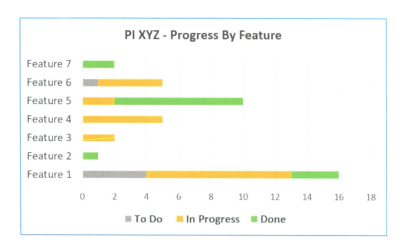

Another Progress By Feature View

To build the Progress By Feature chart, or PI Burnup chart, you will need data similar to the following:

Feature	Stories	Points	To-Do	In-Progress	Done	%Done
Feature 1	2	2	0	0	2	100%
Feature 2	1	5	0	0	5	100%
Feature 3	4	19	3	5	11	58%
Feature 4	3	9	4	0	5	56%
Feature 5	15	93	42	16	35	38%
Feature 6	11	38	25	0	13	34%
Feature 7	5	12	0	8	4	33%
Feature 8	7	16	5	8	3	19%
Feature 9	5	12	4	0	0	0%
Feature 10	3	9	0	0	0	0%

Feature Progress Dataset

114

For those using the popular Jira tool for managing their projects, you can obtain a similar dataset using the 2-D filter gadget on a Jira dashboard, with a query like:

IssueType = Story and epic_link in (XYZ-0100, XYZ-0101, XYZ-0102, etc)

The assumption here is that Jira 'epics' are being used to represent 'features'. The difference in results is that the report will be based on a story count and not on story points. Thus the resulting column chart showing percent done by feature will not include the 'weighting factor' that story points represent. However, this can still be a quick way to produce a valuable summary of progress.

Program-Level Inspect and Adapt

In SAFe, the final iteration of each Program Increment is devoted to Innovation & Planning (IP). The IP iteration culminates in an Inspect & Adapt (I&A) event which includes a demo of all of the objectives delivered in the PI, a scoring of those objectives by business stakeholders, and finally a PI retrospective and problem-solving workshop. This I&A event is the program-level equivalent of scrum's sprint review and retrospective, and serves the same purpose. The event takes place typically on the last day of the IP Iteration, which is the day immediately before the PI Planning event for the next PI. Inspect and Adapt (I&A) activities also run throughout the Program Increment as a faster inner loop to ensure a timely reaction to problems or opportunities as they present themselves.

Integrating Scrum into SAFe

Scrum teams that are part of an Agile Release Train (ART), and are working to deliver SAFe Program Increments, operate in a much broader context than that of a sole scrum team working from a single product backlog. All of the team's core work practices: Sprint Planning, Daily Scrums, Sprint Reviews and Retrospectives, will need to take into account the broader context of the current Program Increment, and its associated PI Objectives. They will need to interact with additional roles defined by the SAFe framework, and will need to be familiar with additional artifacts defined by SAFe. We will take a look at each of scrum's key events and see what additional considerations might be appropriate for teams operating within a SAFe Agile Release Train.

Backlog Refinement. Backlog refinement is an activity used by scrum teams to get backlog items *ready* for development. In particular, user stories should ideally have:

- who/what/why defined
- acceptance criteria
- small enough to fit in a single sprint – split if necessary
- dependencies identified and resolved or mitigated
- estimated in story points

In scrum, we have a single product backlog, owned and managed by a single Product Owner. A scrum PO is the Voice of the Customer and is responsible for all product-related questions including functional requirements, non-functional requirements, priorities and tradeoff decisions. In the SAFe framework, product requirements may originate in response to strategic initiatives formulated at the Portfolio Level. Once epics have been sufficiently defined, ranked and approved, they are then elaborated further into features which are maintained in a Program Backlog. The Program Backlog is equivalent to the scrum product backlog, but is shared between all of the teams making up an Agile Release Train. Initial refinement of items from the Program Backlog into user stories happens during a PI Planning event. During PI Planning however, there is not usually enough time available to craft user stories into a full definition of ready, and these initial set of stories may be fairly crude one-line summaries of intended behavior, requiring further refinement later during backlog refinement. It is important during backlog refinement to keep a watch on any additional scope or demands on development capacity that may impact the PI Objectives of the program, and to ensure that these issues and any necessary tradeoffs are addressed promptly.

Sprint Planning. Sprint Planning is a 2-part event that addresses:

1. Confirm what can be delivered in the upcoming sprint
2. Identify the work needed to deliver the increment

The 'what' part of planning for a specific iteration has already been answered to a large extent in the team breakout sessions during PI Planning. In sprint planning however, the team will need to nail down the details of what will be done and how to do it. Inevitably, additional requirements may emerge as details are elaborated further, and these may impact the team's overall ability to deliver on their target PI objectives. Team's may need to get creative in finding more economical ways to deliver on those objectives. Any necessary scope changes or trade-offs will need to be reviewed with the broader program, and this should be done immediately so that appropriate actions can be taken to ensure that value delivered by the release train as a whole is maximized.

Daily Scrum. This event is where the team updates themselves on progress in the last 24 hours, and then aligns on a plan for the next 24 hours that they believe keeps them on track to achieve the sprint goal. The sprint plan may be tweaked and adjusted throughout the sprint to ensure that the sprint goal is achieved, or at least that maximum possible value is delivered. If the purpose of the stand-up includes some level of re-planning, then teams need to be aware of each other's progress and delays. A scrum-of-scrums (or 'ART Sync') can be used to synchronize the work of multiple of teams, enabling teams to stay aligned and to adjust their plans based on the other teams' progress. Having good visibility into the state of the overall program using radiators like a program wall-board is invaluable for keeping teams synchronized on goals and progress at both team and program levels. Impediments and risks that have the potential to impact the overall program must be escalated promptly to the program team for resolution or at least mitigation. Transparency is key, and bad news can become worse news if delayed. The program team should be focused on optimizing the value delivered from the overall ART, and needs visibility of risks or impediments from all teams.

Sprint Review. The Sprint Review is an event held at the end of every sprint to inspect the latest increment and adapt the Product Backlog if needed. The event is attended by the Scrum Team and stakeholders. The SAFe framework recommends holding a system-level demo at the end of each iteration, the focus of which is to demonstrate fully integrated features or end-to-end operation of a system. One major practical challenge is getting stakeholders to commit to sitting through multiple team-level demos and then an additional system-level demo. The best option, in practical terms, might be to hold a single event, where all teams from the ART demonstrate their completed work, and then have a demonstration any new system-level functionality at the end. Having all teams and all stakeholders in the same place at the same time can help ensure that critical feedback is received and acted upon.

Sprint Retrospective. The Sprint Retrospective is held at the end of every sprint and is an opportunity for the Scrum Team to inspect itself and create a plan for improvements to be enacted during the next sprint. As teams strive to improve their agility and develop an agile mindset they should be deriving ultimate guidance from the 4 Values and 12 Principles of the Agile Manifesto. For example, the first principle states: Our highest priority is to satisfy the customer through early and continuous delivery of valuable software. Teams should be asking themselves whether their work is consistent with this principle at the conclusion of each sprint, and if not, what improvements they can make to move closer to this goal. At the end of each Program Increment (PI), the ART will conduct and Inspect & Adapt session to evaluate how well the PI objectives were implemented (PI System Demo) followed by a Problem Solving workshop to conduct root cause analysis on any major misses, together with corrective actions or improvements for the next PI. The Inspect & Adapt session typically happens the day before the next PI Planning event. If the teams have been conducting effective sprint retrospectives throughout the PI, no major surprises should be expected. However the Inspect & Adapt event is a great opportunity for all teams on the release train to share their experiences and learning so that the performance of the entire ART can be systematically improved from PI to PI.

PI Execution Checklist:

- Scrum of Scrums meets on a regular cadence, and is effective at aligning the team on progress, risks, adjustments.
- Effective use of information radiators is made to make the program plan is visible and easy to understand, ensure team alignment and to identify program risks as early as possible.
- PI scope is proactively managed. Adjustments are made at iteration boundaries.
- A system demo is held at the end of every iteration.
- RTE is effective at facilitating all program ceremonies, and reporting progress.

Final Thoughts

I have attempted to show that it is possible, using only a small subset of the SAFe framework, to set up a system that delivers value continuously with solid alignment between business stakeholders and delivery teams. Lean and agile principles are the most important sources of guidance while building an initial version of the framework for your organization. Inspect and adapt cycles are the means to continuously improve. The transformation of business strategies into working products on a continuous basis while preserving the maximum flexibility to pivot in response to business conditions is what is being sought.

Your first PI Planning event may feel a bit chaotic, and that's just how this strange event should feel! Don't be afraid to try and not completely succeed. This is where the learning happens. If you have the opportunity, observe other PI Planning events at other organizations within your company. Another thing to try is to keep your first PI short, say 3 iterations, and treat it as a learning exercise, so you can *fail fast* and move ahead with new learning. Use the predictability metric to track progress in both planning and execution.

Someone at SAFE Inc. said "There is no magic in SAFE, except PI Planning". I fully agree. This is perhaps SAFe's secret sauce. If well planned and facilitated, business stakeholders and delivery teams should emerge from a PI Planning event completely aligned on business outcomes and priorities for the next 10-week timebox based on a reasonably solid plan. The event may not involve any sorcery, but it certainly produces a huge amount of organizational energy and synergy.

About The Author

Liam Kane is a SAFe Program Consultant (SPC) and experienced agile coach, and works to help companies navigate the transition to agility at scale. Liam is a subject matter expert in Agile, Scrum, Lean, Kanban, and SAFe.

Prior to agile consulting, Liam held director-level positions in software product development, and has worked for companies both small and large in Europe, Asia and the USA.

Liam holds a Ph. D. in Physics from Queen's University Belfast, N. Ireland.

He lives in the Boston area, and can be contacted via his LinkedIn profile:

https://www.linkedin.com/in/kaneliam/

Recommended Reading

1. *Lean Thinking*, James P. Womack and Daniel T. Jones, (Simon and Schuster, 1996, 2003)
2. *The Lean Startup,* Eric Reis, Crown Business, 2011
3. *The Principles of Product Development Flow,* Donald G. Reinertsen, Celeritas Publishing, 2009
4. *Kanban and Scrum, Making The Best of Both,* Henrik Kniberg and Mattias Skarin, C4Media Inc., 2010
5. *Crossing The Chasm,* Geoffrey A. Moore, Harper Business, 2014
6. *The Lean Product Playbook,* Dan Olsen, Wiley, 2015
7. *User Story Mapping*, Jeff Patton with Peter Economy, O'Reilly, 2014
8. *Leading Change,* John P. Kotter, Harvard Business Press, 1996.
9. *Competitive Strategy. Techniques for Analyzing Industries and Competitors*, Michael E. Porter, The Free Press.

Index

Agile Release Train, 116, 117

ART-Sync, 92

Backlog Refinement, 116

burn-up chart, 111, 112

business agility, 8, 49

confidence vote, 70, 88, 89, 96, 97

Daily Scrum, 118

Delivery Team, 8, 17

empirical, 7

Epic Owner, 25, 62

Epics, 15, 20, 21, 22, 24, 25, 34, 35, 36, 37, 41, 42, 43, 44, 54

feature completion chart, 112

Features, 21

Fibonacci, 58, 63

inspect and adapt, 7, 105

Kanban, 17, 20, 26, 27, 28, 34, 43, 48, 51, 54, 57, 59, 60, 61, 66, 105, 125, 127

Lean, 18, 26, 29, 36, 52, 54, 123, 125, 127

minimum viable product, 16, 72

MVP, 16, 43, 72, 74

PDCA, 16, 29, 103, 105, 107

PI Objectives, 70, 80, 85, 89, 93, 94, 99, 100, 116, 117

Portfolio Backlog, 20, 34, 42, 43, 54, 55, 62

Portfolio Management, 8, 13, 15, 33, 37, 52, 54

Predictability Metric, 93

Product Manager, 25, 60, 61, 62

Product Owner, 25, 60, 117

program backlog, 17, 55, 56, 57, 58, 62, 63, 66, 67, 79, 85, 92, 99

Program Management, 8, 16

Program Wall Board, 81, 90, 92, 99, 100

Risk Assessments, 86

Scrum-Of-Scrums, 62, 92, 105, 106, 109

SMART, 86, 93

Sprint Planning, 105, 116, 117

Sprint Retrospective, 105, 119

Sprint Review, 105, 119

Stories, 21, 22, 25, 31, 69, 71, 72, 90

story mapping, 59, 72, 73

Value Stream, 27, 34

WSJF, 42, 44, 46, 54, 58, 63, 66

This page is intentionally left blank

This page is intentionally left blank

This page is intentionally left blank

This page is intentionally left blank

This page is intentionally left blank

Printed in Great Britain
by Amazon

60782344R00076